First Ladies

Grace Coolidge

Joanne Mattern

ABDO
Publishing Company

visit us at
www.abdopublishing.com

Published by ABDO Publishing Company, 8000 West 78th Street, Edina, Minnesota 55439.
Copyright © 2008 by Abdo Consulting Group, Inc. International copyrights reserved in all
countries. No part of this book may be reproduced in any form without written permission from the
publisher. The Checkerboard Library™ is a trademark and logo of ABDO Publishing Company.

Printed in the United States.

Cover Photo: Corbis
Interior Photos: Corbis pp. 5, 6, 8, 10, 13, 16, 17, 19, 21, 25, 26, 27, 31; Courtesy the Forbes
    Library, Northampton, Massachusetts pp. 7, 9; Getty Images pp. 12, 15; Library of Congress
    pp. 11, 22, 23

Series Coordinator: BreAnn Rumsch
Editors: Rochelle Baltzer, BreAnn Rumsch
Art Direction & Cover Design: Neil Klinepier

Library of Congress Cataloging-in-Publication Data

Mattern, Joanne, 1963-
  Grace Coolidge / Joanne Mattern.
      p. cm. -- (First ladies)
  Includes index.
  ISBN-13: 978-1-59928-793-5
  1. Coolidge, Grace Goodhue, 1879-1957--Juvenile literature. 2. Presidents' spouses--United
States--Biography--Juvenile literature. I. Title.
  E792.1.C6M38 2007
  973.91'5092--dc22
  [B]
                                                                              2007009728

Contents

Grace Coolidge

Grace Coolidge was a much admired First Lady. Her husband, Calvin Coolidge, was the thirtieth president of the United States. He served as president from 1923 to 1929.

Mr. and Mrs. Coolidge were very different from each other. In fact, people often wondered how they had ended up together. Mr. Coolidge was quiet, serious, and shy. But, Mrs. Coolidge loved to talk and laugh. She had a lot of friends, too. Despite these differences, they loved each other and had a strong marriage.

Mrs. Coolidge was First Lady during a time of great **prosperity** in the United States. In the 1920s, Americans enjoyed a booming **economy** and many new inventions, such as the radio. Mrs. Coolidge's lively personality made her a favorite First Lady during an exciting time in American history.

During her husband's presidency, Grace Coolidge was known as the most popular First Lady since Dolley Madison. Mrs. Madison was married to James Madison, the fourth president of the United States.

A Lively Child

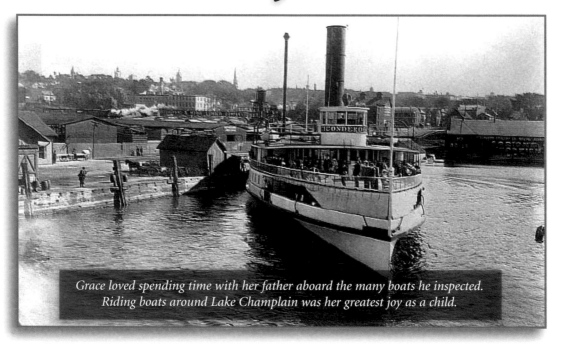

Grace loved spending time with her father aboard the many boats he inspected. Riding boats around Lake Champlain was her greatest joy as a child.

Grace Anna Goodhue was born in Burlington, Vermont, on January 3, 1879. Burlington was a small but busy city on the shores of Lake Champlain. Steamboats and other ships traveled there from New York, which is on the other side of the lake. Boats arrived from other parts of Vermont, too.

Grace as a child

Grace was the only child of Andrew and Lemira Barrett Goodhue. They loved her very much. Andrew worked as a steamboat inspector. Lemira cared for Grace and their home on Maple Street.

Even as a baby, Grace always seemed to be smiling and enjoying life. But as she grew, she developed spine problems. So, she performed exercises to strengthen her back. Still, Grace had a happy, outgoing personality.

Grace started school when she was five years old. She attended classes in a small, brick schoolhouse near her home. Later, Grace went to Burlington High School, where she was a popular student. She graduated in 1897.

College Life

In 1898, Grace entered the University of Vermont in Burlington. Since the school was close, Grace lived at home during her college years.

Grace kept busy throughout her time at college. She sang in the university choir and acted in plays. She was also student vice president her second year. Grace worked hard at school and made many friends. She was always ready to have fun!

Burlington's landscape provided Grace and her friends with plenty of recreation.

In the summers, Grace and her friends had picnics together. They also went sailing and swimming at Lake Champlain. In the winters, they went ice-skating on the lake and sledding down Burlington's steep hills. And, Grace and her friends often rode in horse-driven sleighs to get to parties and dances.

In spring 1902, Grace graduated from college. A family friend told Grace about the Clarke School for the **Deaf** in Northampton, Massachusetts. The school needed teachers. Grace liked the idea of teaching deaf children. So that fall, she went to Northampton to train for her new job.

Grace was never hard to miss at school. People often heard her loud laugh as she walked around the school grounds.

A Funny Meeting

Grace felt her work at the Clarke School was very important. She was a wonderful teacher who enjoyed helping her students learn new things. Grace remained interested in education for the **deaf** throughout her life.

One morning at the school, Grace noticed a young man through a window. He was in a house across the street, shaving in a hat and long underwear! Grace thought he looked funny and burst out laughing. The funny young man was Calvin Coolidge. When he heard Grace's laugh, he decided he wanted to meet her.

Calvin was from Vermont, just like Grace. But, they were very different from each other. Grace was lively and outgoing. Calvin was reserved and quiet. He was also seven years older than Grace. Many people wondered what they had in common. Grace told her friends that she and Calvin understood each other.

Calvin didn't think he needed a wife. But, he quickly changed his mind after he met Grace!

Calvin was a respected lawyer in Northampton. He was also interested in politics and history. Calvin enjoyed being with Grace. She showed him how much fun life could be. The couple enjoyed going for drives, walking in the woods, and attending church picnics.

Helen Keller, a fellow supporter of the Clarke School, would place her fingers over Grace's mouth to read her lips.

Hearing Miracles

The Clarke School for the Deaf first opened its doors in 1867. It was the first school of its kind to teach deaf children to speak. Today, the school has more than 500 students at five locations. It has become a recognized leader in the field of oral education. This type of education allows students with a hearing disability to work, play, and attend school.

Today, the Clarke School continues to teach deaf students to speak and read lips. However, the school also uses many devices that support hearing-impaired people. These resources include tutors and translators, closed captioning for television, and hearing aids.

More advanced technologies include Communication Access Realtime Translation (CART). This system translates spoken words into written words. There are also medical technologies, such as hearing devices that can be surgically placed in the ear.

Many people have contributed to the Clarke School's success. Mrs. Coolidge continued her loyalty to the school throughout her life by serving on the Board of Trustees. Mrs. Coolidge also developed a deep friendship with author and teacher Helen Keller, who was herself blind and deaf.

Married Life

In 1905, Calvin told Grace he wanted to marry her. She happily said yes. However, Grace's mother wanted her to wait one year.

Their first home remained a special place for Grace and Calvin throughout their lives.

Lemira told Calvin that Grace should learn to bake bread first. But, Calvin told Grace's mother that he could buy bread at a store. He wanted to marry Grace right away.

Eventually, Lemira gave in. Calvin and Grace were married on October 4, 1905. The wedding took place in Grace's childhood house. Soon, the couple moved into a **duplex** in Northampton. Calvin worked at his law office in town. And, Grace left her job at the Clarke School to care for their home.

Calvin was proud of his wife. "She is going to be a great help to me," he told people. On September 7, 1906, Calvin and Grace's first son was born. They named him John after Calvin's father. Then on April 13, 1908, the Coolidges had a second son. They named him Calvin Jr.

Meanwhile, Calvin was becoming an important politician in town. Grace was always at her husband's side. She also was active in church and community activities. The Coolidges soon became one of Northampton's most admired and popular families.

In the early 1900s, most married women did not work outside of the home.

An Important Man

In 1909, Mr. Coolidge was elected mayor of Northampton. His popularity led to his reelection the following year. As mayor, Mr. Coolidge worked hard to help the town save money. And, he showed a special interest in education. He made sure Northampton's teachers received fair pay.

Mr. Coolidge continued to succeed in politics. In 1911, he became a state senator for Massachusetts. Later, he became president of the state senate. He had to move to Boston for this job. But, Mrs. Coolidge and the children stayed in Northampton. They looked forward to his visits each weekend.

In 1914, a man named Frank Waterman Stearns heard Mr. Coolidge speak in front of the state senate. Mr. Stearns was an important merchant in Boston. And, he agreed with Mr. Coolidge's ideas. He encouraged Mr. Coolidge to run for **lieutenant governor** of Massachusetts. Mr. Stearns helped him campaign and raise money.

The next year, Mr. Coolidge won the election. In 1918, he was elected governor of Massachusetts. While Mr. Coolidge focused on his career, Mrs. Coolidge raised their boys. She also supported the **Red Cross** during **World War I**.

Though Mr. Coolidge was often busy working, he spent time with his family in Vermont every July. There, Mrs. Coolidge enjoyed the fresh mountain air. And, John and Calvin Jr. helped their grandfather on his farm.

Washington

Mr. Stearns continued to campaign for Governor Coolidge. By 1920, many people wanted Mr. Coolidge to run for president of the United States. Warren G. Harding won the nomination instead. But, Mr. Coolidge agreed to be Mr. Harding's **running mate**.

Mrs. Coolidge was surprised at her husband's decision. She worried that leaving Northampton would be hard on their family. But, Mr. Coolidge wanted to be vice president. So, Mrs. Coolidge supported his decision. In 1920, Mr. Harding and Mr. Coolidge won the election.

In 1921, the Coolidge family moved to Washington, D.C. Suddenly, Mrs. Coolidge became a figure of national importance. She was comfortable in front of people and

Many people wore campaign buttons to show their support for Mr. Harding and Mr. Coolidge.

happy to be at her husband's side. Being the vice president's wife would be a new challenge. But she was ready.

Caring for her sons and the family's apartment kept Mrs. Coolidge busy. But, she also worked hard to help her husband. Mrs. Coolidge contributed to many charities. And, she attended political and government events with the vice president. Soon, her sense of humor made her the most popular woman in Washington, D.C.

As the vice president's wife, Mrs. Coolidge learned how to entertain large groups. Her outgoing, friendly attitude made her guests feel at ease.

Shocking News

In 1923, President Harding became very sick. That July, the Coolidges were visiting Mr. Coolidge's father in Plymouth Notch, Vermont. Just before midnight on August 2, a message arrived at the house. The message said that President Harding had died. Now, Vice President Coolidge would become the president of the United States.

The Coolidges were shocked by the news. President Harding's death was a surprise to everyone. Mrs. Coolidge cried, and she and Mr. Coolidge asked for some quiet time together. Then, they got dressed in their best clothes. Reporters and government officials came to the house to find out what the vice president would do.

Mr. Coolidge asked his father to administer the presidential oath. He did this because his father was a **notary public**. Mrs. Coolidge stood beside her husband as he took the oath. Just before three o'clock in the morning on August 3, Mr. Coolidge became the nation's thirtieth president. Then, he told everyone good night and went back to bed. The Coolidges knew their lives had changed forever.

Mr. Coolidge was the sixth vice president to gain the presidential office because of a president's death.

First Lady

Mrs. Coolidge had faith that her husband could handle the huge responsibilities of being president. And, her commitment to the president helped him do his job well. Yet as First Lady, Mrs. Coolidge felt the demands of public life.

President Coolidge believed that the president and First Lady should set an example for the country. He also felt they should be **conservative**. So, he said Mrs. Coolidge should not wear the short skirts that were in fashion. He also did not approve of the short hairstyles that were popular at the time.

Still, Mrs. Coolidge had fun being First Lady. She and President Coolidge made hundreds of public appearances together. The First Lady hosted numerous parties and other social events. She also invited children to the White House.

Most people still thought the Coolidges made an odd couple. The president was often called "Silent Cal" because he did not like to talk much. However, Mrs. Coolidge's playful personality complemented her husband's quiet disposition.

The First Lady also helped the American people better understand her husband. So, the nation liked President Coolidge, and they loved the First Lady. The White House staff even called her "Sunshine."

Mrs. Coolidge filled the White House with close to 30 pets!
Her most famous pet was a raccoon named Rebecca.

Overcoming Sorrow

In July 1924, tragedy struck the Coolidge family. Calvin Jr. blistered his foot while playing tennis. The blister became infected, and the infection spread through his whole body. Calvin Jr. was rushed to the hospital for an emergency operation. However, he died on July 7.

The Coolidges were deeply saddened. For the first time, the First Lady found it difficult to laugh and be cheerful. Thousands of Americans wrote sympathy letters to the family. Mrs. Coolidge tried to answer as many of the letters as she could. Slowly, life returned to normal.

Life was never the same for the Coolidges after Calvin Jr. (left) *passed away.*

In 1924, Mr. Coolidge ran for president and won. So, Mrs. Coolidge continued her busy role as First Lady. She invited many women's groups to the White House. She especially liked meeting

teachers and nurses. The Coolidges also hosted hundreds of dinners and welcomed many foreign officials.

Americans enjoyed several years of **prosperity** while the Coolidges ran the White House. The president supported laws that helped businesses grow. Many Americans could afford to buy nice things. They thought life had never been better!

The Beeches

In 1929, Mr. Coolidge's presidency ended. So, he and Mrs. Coolidge decided to return to Northampton. They moved back into the **duplex** they had lived in when they were first married. However, the neighbors complained about too many visitors. So in 1930, Mr. and Mrs. Coolidge bought a house that offered more privacy. They called the property "the Beeches."

The Coolidges enjoyed a quiet life at their new home. Mr. Coolidge wrote magazine and newspaper articles. Mrs. Coolidge wrote too, and she took care of the house. "You just can't imagine how good it is," she once said of life at the Beeches.

Unfortunately, the couple did not have much time together. Mr. Coolidge's heart began to fail, so he was often weak and tired. On January 5, 1933, Mrs. Coolidge went shopping. She returned shortly, and went to tell her husband that lunch was ready. But, she was shocked to find that he was dead.

Mr. Coolidge was just 60 years old when he died of a heart attack. The nation shared Mrs. Coolidge's sorrow over the former president's death. Mr. Coolidge's funeral was held in Northampton. He was buried near his childhood home in Plymouth Notch.

The nation was shocked when President Coolidge announced he would not seek another term. Herbert and Lou Hoover (right) became the next president and First Lady.

On Her Own

After her husband died, Mrs. Coolidge was very lonely. At first, she lived quietly and did not make many public appearances. Eventually, she began writing articles and poems for women's magazines. Mrs. Coolidge also served on the **Board of Trustees** of the Clarke School for the **Deaf**. And for fun, she often attended Boston Red Sox games.

Mrs. Coolidge also loved to spend time with her son John and his family. During the 1950s, Mrs. Coolidge's heart began to fail. On July 8, 1957, John and his daughters planned to visit her at home. But, she died just 20 minutes before they arrived.

Mrs. Coolidge was a devoted baseball fan. Her favorite team was the Boston Red Sox.

Mrs. Coolidge's funeral was held in Northampton. She was buried in Plymouth Notch, Vermont, near her husband and younger son. A few years later, Mr. Coolidge's childhood home became a national historic site.

There, people can visit the home and see where Mr. Coolidge took the presidential oath. They are also reminded of the important role his wife played in his success. Mrs. Coolidge dedicated her life to being a supportive mother, wife, and First Lady. She faced her responsibilities with enthusiasm. Today, Grace Coolidge is remembered as one of America's most charming First Ladies.

A Place Called Plymouth Notch

Calvin Coolidge was born in a modest house on July 4, 1872, in Plymouth Notch, Vermont. This little village was his childhood home. Yet it played a large role in his political life as well. Today, the village remains carefully preserved for visitors to see where the former president grew up. Plymouth Notch is also where Mr. and Mrs. Coolidge are buried.

The Calvin Coolidge Visitor Center is home to a small museum. It features information about President Coolidge's career. And, a changing exhibit displays gifts the president received while in office. Important moments are highlighted at several other buildings at the site, including:

•The Coolidge Homestead, where Mr. Coolidge took the presidential oath at 2:47 AM on August 3, 1923.

•The Calvin Coolidge Birthplace, which is attached to the general store.

•Coolidge Hall, a dance hall above the general store, where President Coolidge created his summer presidential office in 1924.

Timeline

1879	Grace Anna Goodhue was born on January 3.
1897	Grace graduated from Burlington High School.
1898–1902	Grace attended the University of Vermont.
1902–1905	Grace taught classes at the Clarke School for the Deaf.
1905	Grace married Calvin Coolidge on October 4.
1906	The Coolidges' son John was born on September 7.
1908	The Coolidges' son Calvin Jr. was born on April 13.
1909	Mr. Coolidge was elected mayor of Northampton, Massachusetts.
1911	Mr. Coolidge was elected as a state senator for Massachusetts.
1915	Mr. Coolidge was elected lieutenant governor of Massachusetts.
1918	Mr. Coolidge was elected governor of Massachusetts.
1921–1923	Mr. Coolidge served as U.S. vice president.
1923–1929	Mrs. Coolidge acted as First Lady, while her husband served as president.
1924	Calvin Jr. died from an infection.
1930	The Coolidges moved to the Beeches.
1933	Mr. Coolidge died of a heart attack on January 5.
1957	Mrs. Coolidge died of heart failure on July 8.

Did You Know?

During college, Grace helped start a new chapter of a women's society called Pi Beta Phi. The girls held their meetings in the Goodhues' attic.

Mrs. Coolidge loved bright colors, especially red.

Mrs. Coolidge loved baseball, and she could throw better than many men. She taught the game to her sons while their father was away from home.

Mrs. Coolidge made a point of hiking or walking every day. She also loved hobbies such as horseback riding. And, she frequently played the piano during her free time.

Mrs. Coolidge worked to bring back furniture and other items that had been removed from the White House over time. This included Abraham Lincoln's bed!

Mrs. Coolidge was the first First Lady to address the nation by radio. She only gave one address, saying "Good-bye" at the end of her husband's second presidential term.

Mrs. Coolidge's white collie, Rob Roy, is featured in her official White House portrait.

Glossary

board of trustees - a group of people that makes legal decisions about how property, money, or services are given to benefit others.

conservative - a person who has traditional beliefs and often dislikes change.

deaf - wholly or partly unable to hear.

duplex - a two-family house.

economy - the way a nation uses it money, goods, and natural resources.

lieutenant governor - the second-highest executive office in a state government. This official acts as governor should the elected governor become ill or die.

notary public - a person who specializes in making sure legal documents are real and not forged.

prosperity - the condition of being successful or thriving.

Red Cross - an international organization that cares for the sick, wounded, or homeless.

running mate - a candidate running for a lower-rank position on an election ticket, especially the candidate for vice president.

World War I - from 1914 to 1918, fought in Europe. Great Britain, France, Russia, the United States, and their allies were on one side. Germany, Austria-Hungary, and their allies were on the other side.

Web Sites

To learn more about Grace Coolidge, visit ABDO Publishing
Company on the World Wide Web at **www.abdopublishing.com**.
Web sites about Grace Coolidge are featured on our Book Links page.
These links are routinely monitored and updated to provide the most
current information available.

Index